FREE Gift
-for Parents-

51 **SIMPLE STRATEGIES** for **Better Communication** with **Your Child**

www.HelloMulberryAvenue.com

SCAN ME

https://www.hellomulberryavenue.com/51strategies

9-in-1
Better You Zoo

Confident like a Crocodile
Focus like a Fox
Empathy like an Elephant
Lead like a Lion
Helpful like a Honeybee
Polite like a Panda
Cooperate like a Camel
Brave like a Bear
Try like a Tiger

Better You Zoo 9 Books in 1
Published by Mulberry Avenue

by Sonny Swinhart & Sandy Swinhart

www.HelloMulberryAvenue.com

print ISBN: 978-1-957337-16-6
digital ISBN: 978-1-957337-17-3

CONTENT

Confident

like a crocodile

Are you **confident** like a crocodile?

Confidence means keeping
calm & cool
in all situations.

Confidence means **believing in yourself** deep down.

Confidence is
super important.

It can help you
do better in life.

It can help you
feel better in life.

Confidence can help you win.
And it can help you,
if you lose.

Confidence can give
you the special energy
to try.

And if you can try,
you can win.

Without confidence you can feel **scared**,

sometimes for

no reason.

The **confident crocodile** doesn't have that problem.

The confident crocodile walks into every situation with its **head held high.**

The crocodile has **no doubts.**

It knows what it wants.

The crocodile makes every move with a **strong mind.**

The crocodile is **confident** when walking.

The crocodile is **confident** when swimming.

The crocodile is **confident** when looking for dinner.

When the crocodile messes up, it doesn't get down on itself.

It takes a **deep breath** and **tries again**.

So, when you feel

iffy

like an **iguana**...

When you feel

not sure

like a **squirrel...**

When you
hesitate
like a **hedgehog**...

Be **confident**

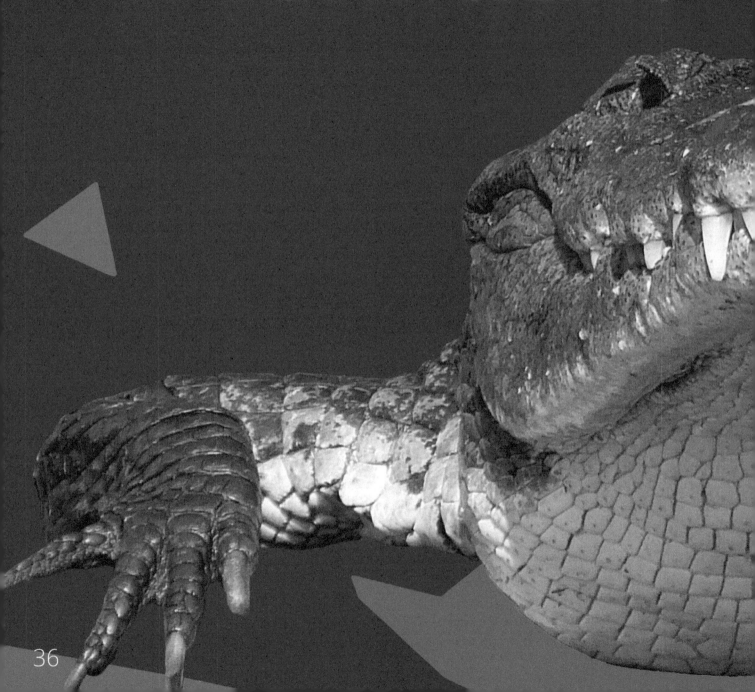

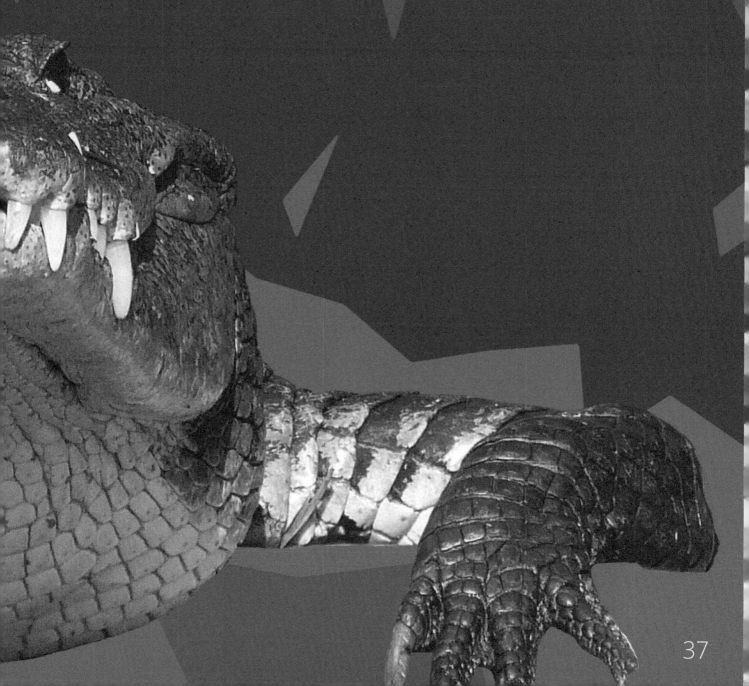

like a **crocodile.**

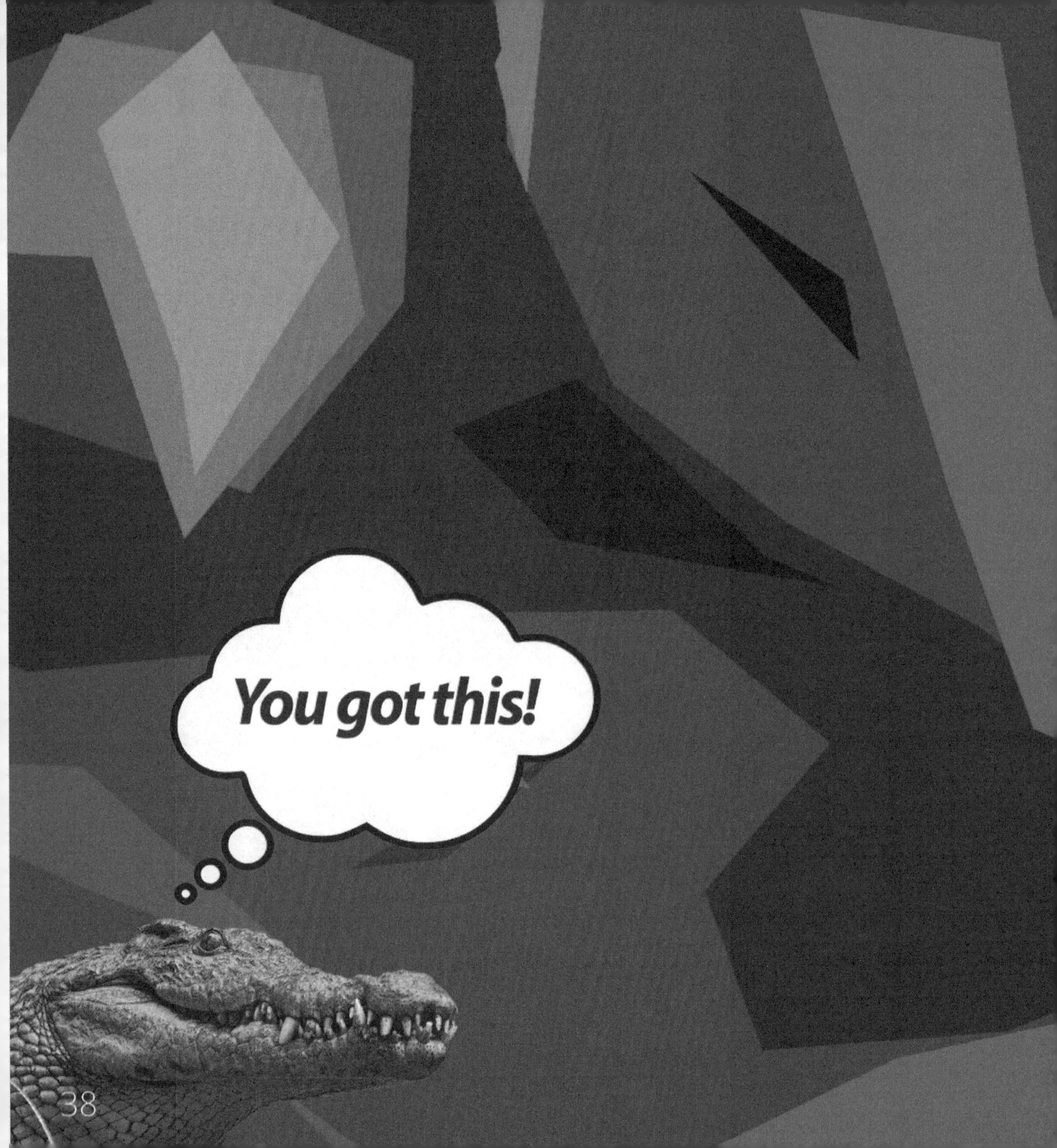
You got this!

Focus
like a fox

Do you focus like a fox?

Having focus means paying **close attention** in all situations.

Having focus means **concentrating** to see clearly.

Focus is **super important.**

It can help you **do better in life.**

It can help you **stay on track.**

Focus can help you

make

smart

decisions.

Without focus you can **waste**

time

and

energy.

The **focused fox** doesn't have that problem.

The focused fox

avoids

distraction.

The fox is focused when **pouncing on prey.**

The fox is focused when **listening.**

The fox is focused when **resting.**

If the fox **messes up**, it doesn't think of giving up.

It just **concentrates** and **keeps trying**.

So, when you feel

disorganized

like a donkey...

When you feel

scattered

like a salamander...

When you feel

mixed-up

like a monkey...

Focus
like a
fox.

Empathy
like an elephant

Do you have **empathy** like an elephant?

Having **empathy** means
you **understand**
how others feel.

Having **empathy** means
you **show others**
that you care.

Empathy is **super important.**

It can help you **make** good friends.

It can help you **keep** good friends.

Empathy is good for understanding those around you.

It can help you build **strong relationships.**

It can help the people around you **feel good** too.

Those who do not show empathy, may seem to be **mean** or like they **do not care.**

Elephants with **empathy** do not have that problem.

The elephant **listens, helps** and **shares happiness.**

The elephant shows **empathy** when

walking in a line.

The elephant shows **empathy** when **helping someone in need.**

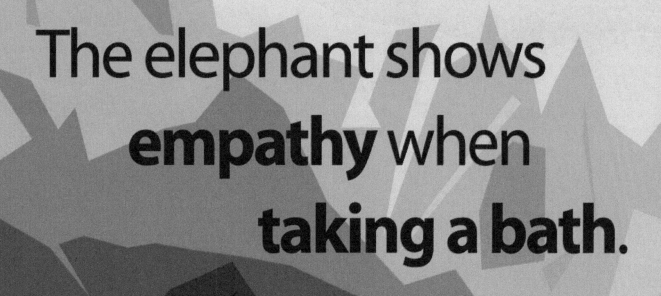

The elephant shows **empathy** when **taking a bath.**

If elephants
have a friend
who needs support,
they help.

So, when you feel

selfish

like a shark...

When you feel

brutal

like a bear...

When you feel

cold

like a crab...

Show **empathy**

like an

elephant.

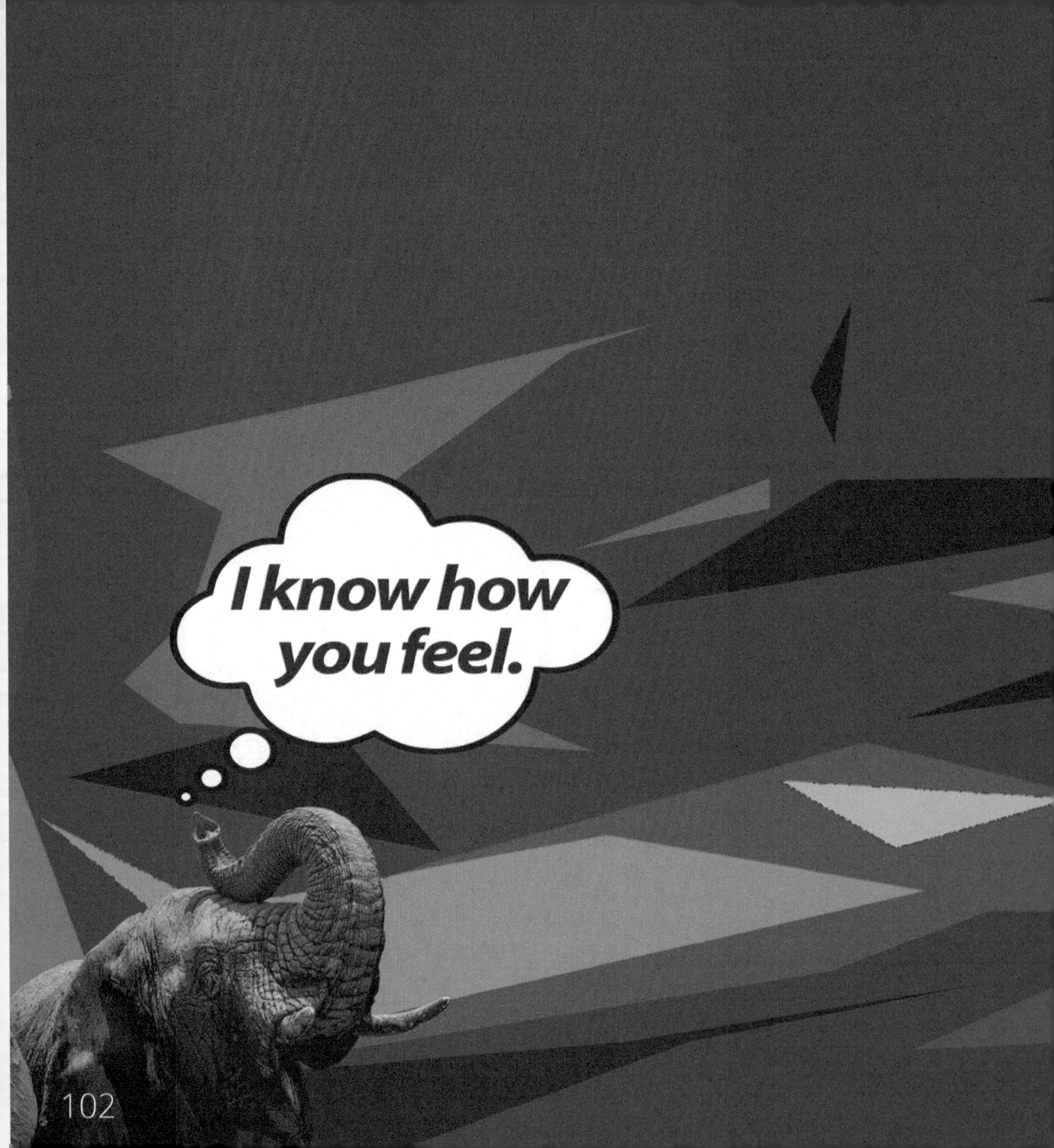
I know how you feel.

Lead
like a lion

Are you a **leader** like a lion?

A leader
takes charge
and
guides.

Leadership is
super important.

It can help you
do good in life.

It can help you
solve problems.

A leader can **help others** do their best.

A leader can **make others strong** too.

Those who cannot lead,
must follow.

Sometimes followers feel **unimportant.**

A lion who leads doesn't have that problem.

The leader lion is **confident.**

It faces difficult **challenges.**

It motivates others to **win.**

The lion is a leader when it **roars.**

The lion is a leader when it **protects its family.**

The lion is a leader when it **hunts for food.**

When lions have a challenge, they focus and help to **do their best.**

So, when you feel

goalless

like a goose...

When you feel
frail

like a finch...

When you feel

meek

like a marmot...

Lead
like a
lion.

Polite
like a panda

Are you polite like a panda?

Being **polite** means you are respectful and considerate to others.

Being **polite** means you mind your manners.

Being **polite** is **super important.**

Being **polite** can help you do well in life,

get what you want

&

get what you need.

Being **polite** can help you make more friends.

Being **polite** can help you feel better about yourself too.

Those who are
not polite are
rude.

Those who are
rude are not
liked very much.

The **polite panda** doesn't have that problem.

The **polite panda** is polite in all situations.

It is friendly and fair to others.

It sits up straight when eating.

It is a good sport and takes turns.

The panda is **polite** when **eating.**

The panda is **polite** when **playing with family.**

The panda is **polite** when **hanging out with friends.**

If the panda is in a hard situation,

it nicely accepts help from others.

So, when you feel

rude

like a rhinoceros...

When you feel

crude

like a crocodile...

When you feel

vulgar

like a vulture...

Be **polite** like a **panda.**

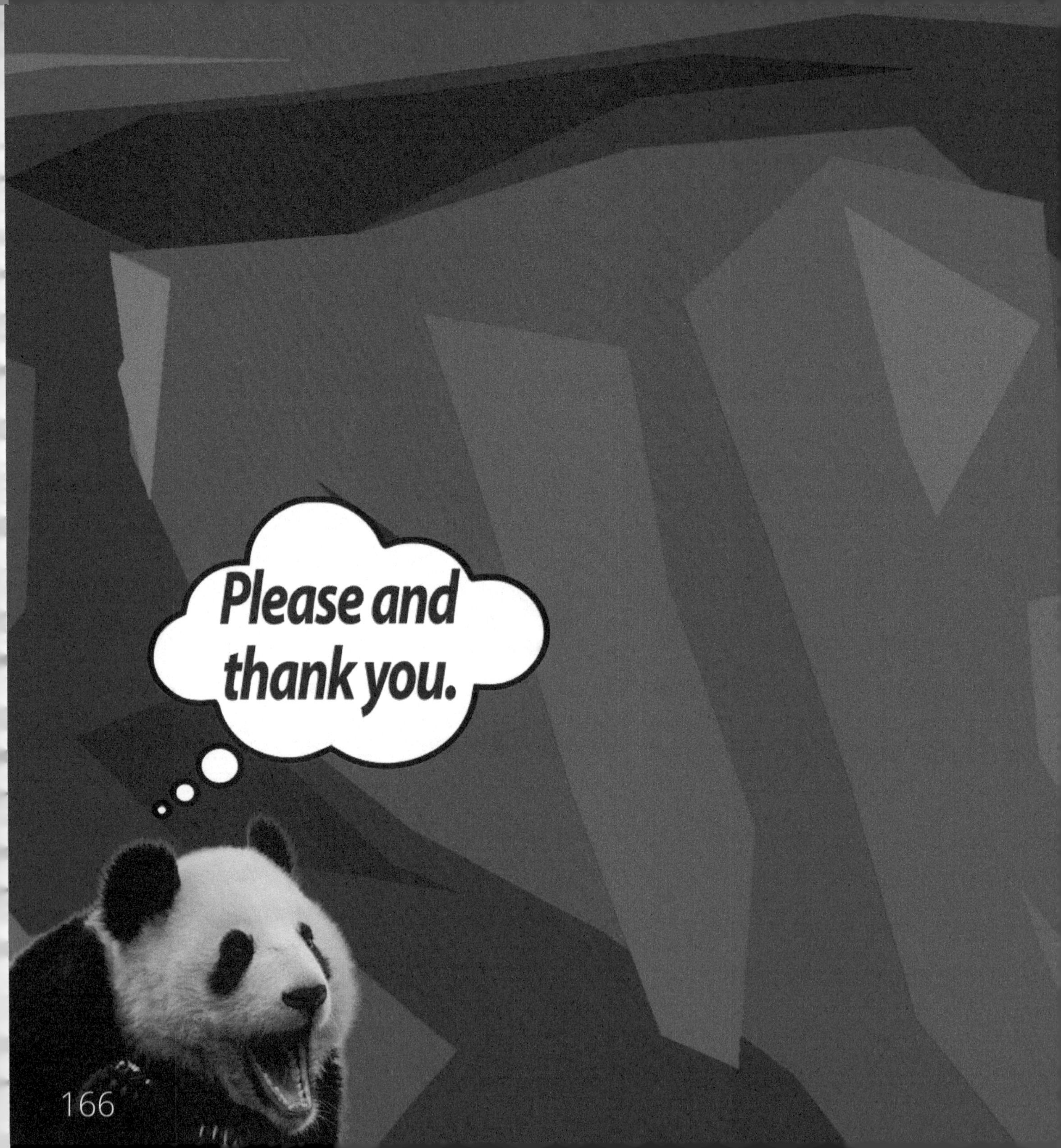
Please and thank you.

Helpful

like a honey bee

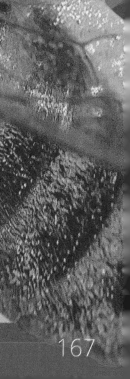

Are you helpful like a honey bee?

Being helpful means **you are useful** to others.

Being helpful means **you make things easier** for others.

Being helpful is **super important.**

It can help you do **good in life.**

It can make you **happier and healthier too.**

Being helpful can help you do good things **for others.**

Being helpful is **good for the community.**

Those who are not helpful are unhelpful.

Being unhelpful can make others upset and might be selfish.

The
helpful honey bee
does
not
have
that
problem.

The helpful honey bee is helpful in all situations.

It gives its energy and time to others when needed.

It does not only think of itself, but others too.

It is productive and shares its work with other bees, animals, and plants.

The honey bee
is helpful
when **flying.**

The honey bee
is helpful
when
working in the hive.

The honey bee
is helpful
when **gathering**
pollen.

When a honey bee is needed, the honey bee can be relied on.

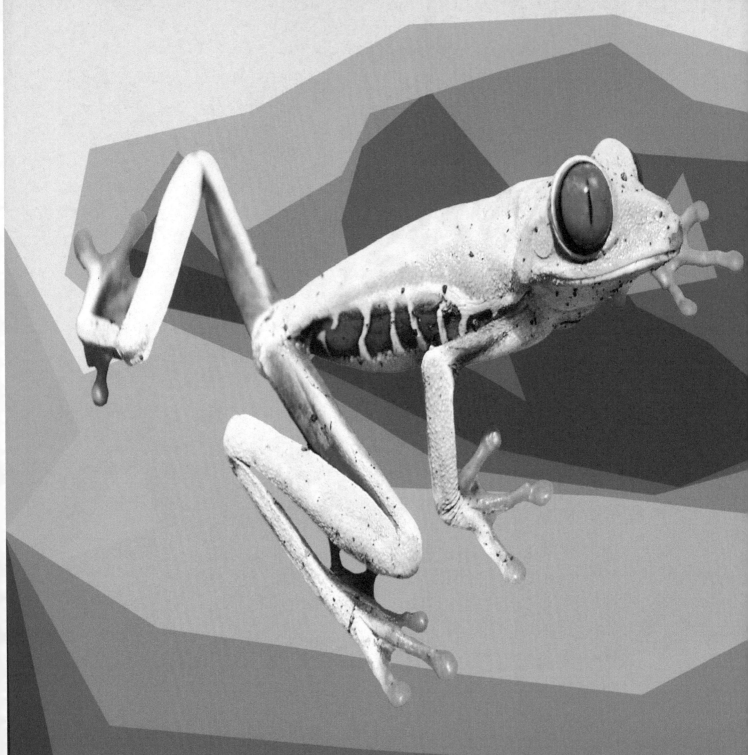

So, when you feel **trivial** like a tree frog...

When you feel
selfish
like a shellfish...

When you feel
disruptive
like a duck...

Be **helpful** like a **honey bee.**

Cooperate

like a camel

Do you cooperate like a camel?

Cooperation means sharing goals with others.

Cooperation means working well with others, too.

Cooperation is **super important.**

It can help others **feel good.**

It ca help you **feel good** too.

Cooperation helps us to **get things done.**

Copperation helps us to **get along.**

Those who
don't cooperate
might **feel alone.**

The camel that cooperates doesn't have that problem.

The camel that cooperates **can get things done.** And its team can do **very well.**

They can have
pride in their team.

They can **share**
skills and abilities.

The camel **cooperates** when **trekking on a long journey.**

The camel **cooperates** when **it's break time.**

The camel **cooperates** when **helping to carry a heavy load.**

The camel is **unique** and has **special** skills it can **share.**

Cooperation makes others **happy.**

So, when you feel **feeble** like a flamingo...

When you resist

like a rat...

When you feel

mean

like a mosquito...

Cooperate
like a
camel.

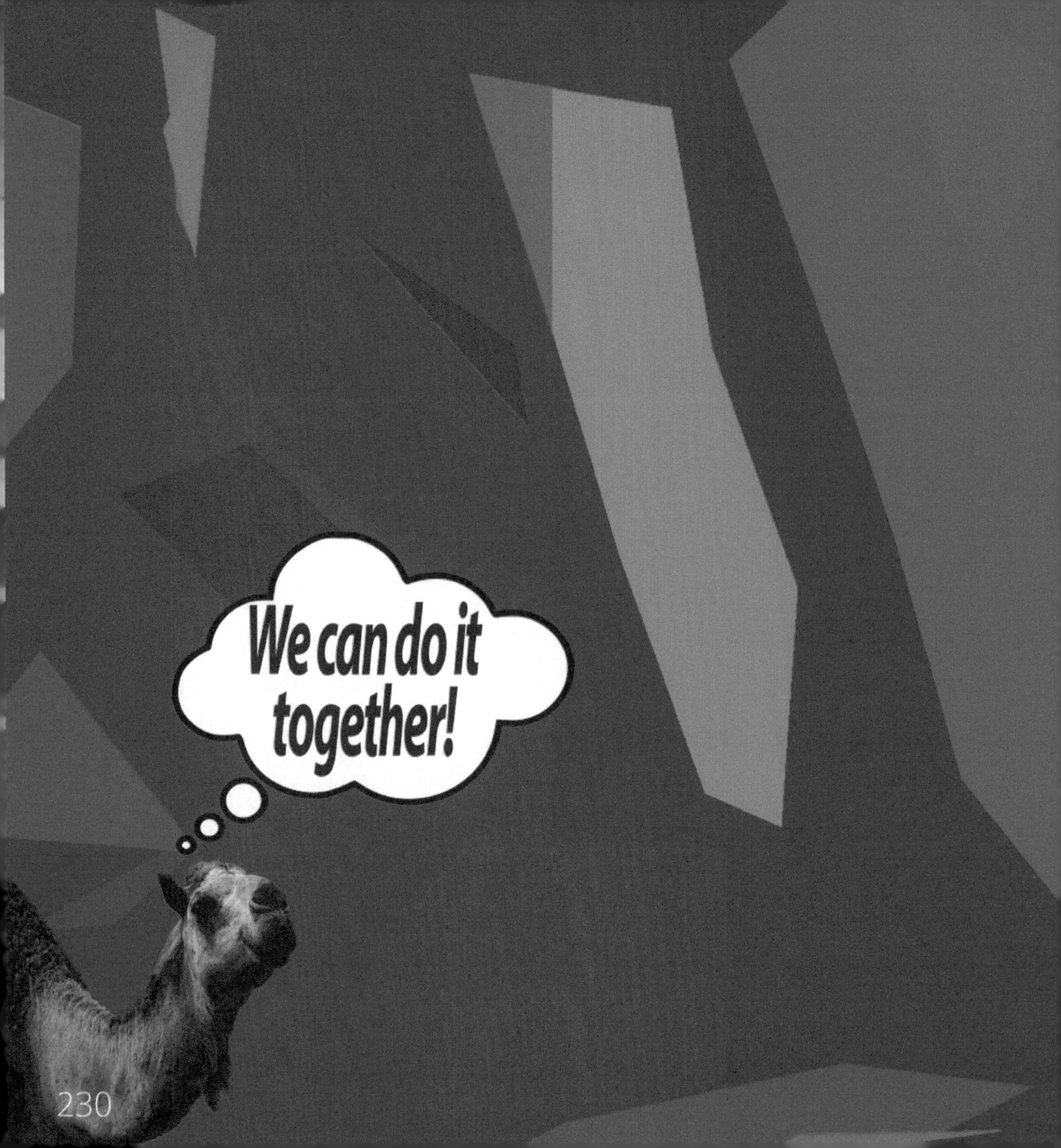
We can do it together!

Brave
like a bear

Are you **brave** like a **bear?**

Being **brave** means facing tough situations.

Being **brave** means having courage when you are scared.

Being brave is **super important.**

It can help you **accomplish** more in life.

Being brave
can help you
beat fear.

Being brave
can help you
try new things.

Being brave
can help you
catch your dreams.

Those who
do not feel brave
are **fearful.**

Those who
are not brave
can get **trapped**
in a place they do not like.

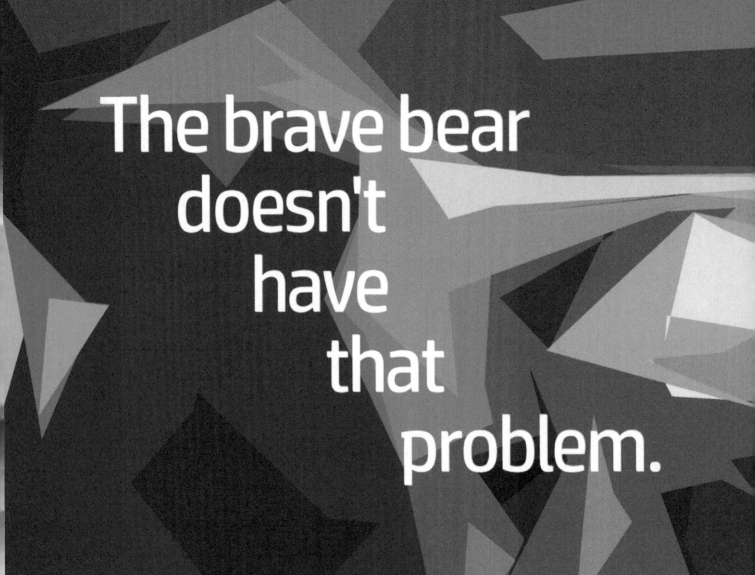

The brave bear doesn't have that problem.

The brave bear is brave in **all situations.**

It will **stand up** for itself.

It is **strong** enough to do what others are too scared to do.

It will not let the size of a problem frighten them.

The bear is **brave** when climbing.

The bear is **brave** when swimming.

The bear is **brave**

when getting
lunch.

If the bear is
challenged,
it will do
what it takes
to get
what it needs.

So, when you
panic
like a penguin...

When you feel
afraid
like an alpaca...

257

When you feel
bashful
like a bunny...

Be **brave** like a **bear.**

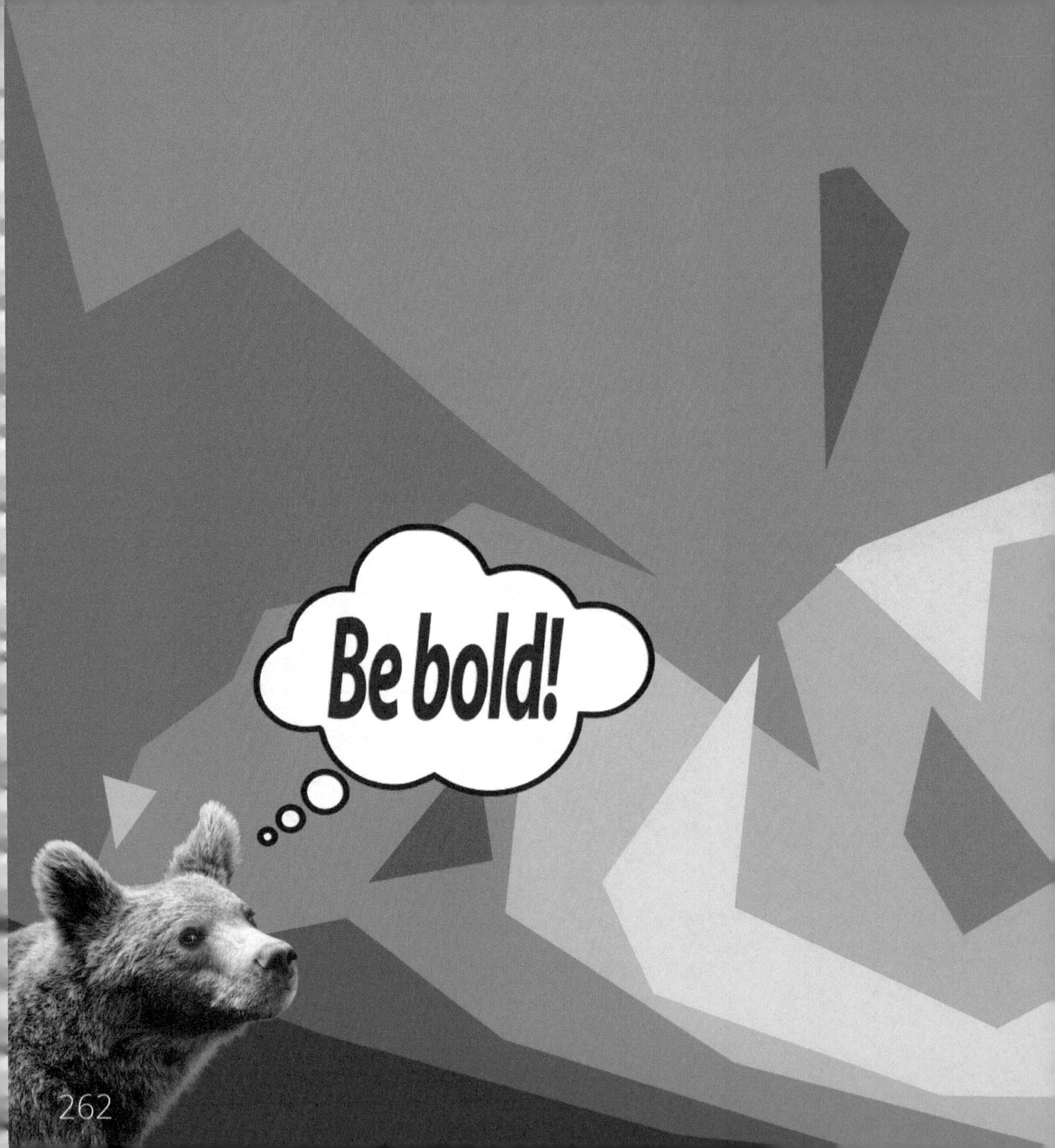
Be bold!

Try like a tiger

Do you **try** like a **tiger?**

Trying means attempting to **complete something**.

Trying means **doing your best** to reach a goal.

Trying is **super important.**

Trying can help you **get things done.**

Trying can help you feel satisfied you finish something.

Trying can help you learn from your mistakes.

Trying will help you be better at what you try.

Those who do not try,
do not finish
and
do not learn new things.

The tiger that tries
does not have
that problem.

The tiger tries
in all situations.

It makes mistakes
and then tries again
and again.

The tiger tries
when
exploring.

The tiger tries when protecting its family.

The tiger tries when playing with friends.

When the tiger fails,
it does not quit.

The tiger tries to learn
from its mistakes.

So, when you feel **lazy** like a **lizard**...

When you feel
hopeless
like a **hyena**...

So, when you feel
pointless
like a **peacock**...

Try
like a
tiger.

Visit the Zoo

SCAN ME

www.hellomulberryavenue.com/byz

Made in the USA
Las Vegas, NV
15 September 2022